To: Emily

From: Mom

Date: Aug. 2013

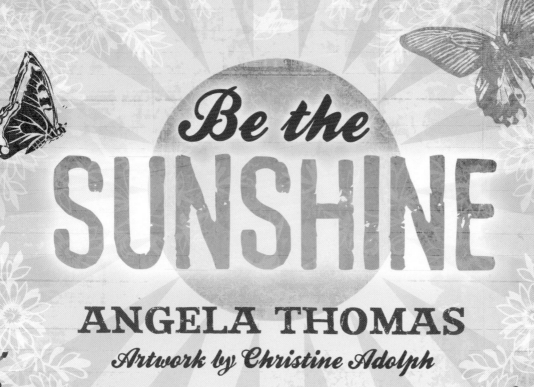

Be the
SUNSHINE

ANGELA THOMAS

Artwork by Christine Adolph

HARVEST HOUSE PUBLISHERS
EUGENE, OREGON

Be the Sunshine

Text copyright © 2013 by Angela Thomas
Artwork copyright © 2013 by Christine Adolph

Published by Harvest House Publishers
Eugene, Oregon 97402
www.harvesthousepublishers.com

ISBN 978-0-7369-5179-1

Artwork designs are reproduced under license from © 2013 by Christine Adolph,
courtesy of MHS Licensing, and may not be reproduced without permission.

Design and production by Franke Design & Illustration, Excelsior, Minnesota

To read more about the sunbeam named Mandy, please visit her website, www.mandyyoung.com.

Printed in China

13 14 15 16 17 18 19 20 21 / LP / 10 9 8 7 6 5 4 3 2 1

For William.
It is my joy to watch you shine.
I love you so,
Your mama

CONTENTS

Be the Sunshine

We are told to let our light shine, and if it does, we won't need to tell anybody it does. Lighthouses don't fire cannons to call attention to their shining—they just shine.

Dwight L. Moody

I am a soccer mom. Bona fide. I have soccer-mom earrings and a soccer-ball bracelet, soccer chairs and a soccer cooler, and all the tailgate accoutrements that make soccer viewing a joy. Nothing makes me happier than sitting in my soccer-mom chair beside a grassy field watching my boy shine.

I'm not sure how it happened, but my boy William was given soccer-boy talent straight from the hand of God. I know his skills came from God because no one else we're related to even knows what a penalty kick is, much less how to play like a fiend.

On a good day, William is a great player and a team leader. He is a true delight to watch. But on this particular afternoon, the visiting team was creaming our team, and my thirteen-year-old son was becoming more and more defeated. As the minutes dragged on, I watched his shoulders slump. He ran at half speed. He didn't run toward the ball or try to energize his teammates. He hung his head as if to say, *Please let this end as soon as possible.*

As his mom, I had had about all I could take. Even though I was in the stands, I could feel my kid giving up. That wasn't what the coach wanted, and it certainly wasn't how we had taught him. I wanted him to keep playing with his heart until the end.

I kept patting my husband's arm and telling him what needed to happen. "The coach just needs to sit William down if he's going to play like that… If he's going to give up when they're down, then maybe he doesn't need to play soccer… I ought to walk out there and tell him we're going home." I was frustrated to say the least.

At one point in the game, the play came to our side of the field. Most of the players had gathered at our side, near the fence in front of our bleachers. During a lull in the game and while the referee was waiting for substitutions, William just happened to be standing at the fence right in front of where I was sitting.

William! Be. The. Sunshine.

I'm telling you, I did not mean to do this. It was not planned. I had no idea it was coming, but from somewhere deep inside my mother's heart, I felt my body stand up, and in front of all the fans and all the players gathered in front of me, I yelled as loud as I could, "William! Be. The. Sunshine."

The moment that last word left my lips, I realized what I had done. All the parents in the stands burst out laughing, and the players smirked and giggled. William never looked at me, but I knew he had heard me because I felt my words land on him. The parents kept roaring and saying things like, "My son would kill me if I yelled something like that!"

My husband leaned over to me, took my hand, and told me with his eyes that it would be a good idea for me to sit down.

After the game was over and we had lost pitifully, William gathered his gear and packed up his athletic bag. Then the cutest soccer boy ever walked straight across the field to me. He kissed me on my cheek, looked into my eyes, and said to me, "Mom, really? 'Be the sunshine'?"

I said, "Oh, honey, I am so sorry. I didn't mean to embarrass you. Truly. It just came right from my mama's heart of love. I couldn't stand watching you be so discouraged. I just wanted you to pick it up and lead your team with enthusiasm. Honey, I promise I will never yell that again. Next time what can I say that would be an encouragement to you?"

"Hmmm. I don't know. Maybe 'go, motor-head.' Something manly."

"You got it, baby. I mean motor-head."

The very next soccer season, we travelled to Charlotte to play a rival school. This time our team was doing the creaming. As our score climbed, we realized that continuing to cheer wildly for our boys would be impolite, so the parents from both schools began talking to each other. One of the dads said something about fourteen-year-old boys entering a new phase where they are embarrassed by everything their parents do. He said, "Just standing there breathing in and out slays them!" We all laughed together about our common dilemma—trying to raise fourteen-year-old boys—and shared stories about embarrassing our sons. Eventually I said, "Oh, I can top that," and I told them about the time I had yelled, "William, be the sunshine!"

One of the more vocal dads from the other team lost it. He said, "Oh, my gosh! I think that is the worst thing I have ever heard. I cannot believe what you yelled to him. My son would never speak to me again if I had done something like that."

I told him I'd felt bad about it for the whole last year, but he was making me feel awful all over again. And then we all laughed about it some more.

Our boys won that day, and as we left the stadium, I ran into the same dad. I said to him, "Great game! Thanks for hosting."

He got this big smile on his face and replied, "Be the sunshine!"

In that moment, I had a flash of brilliance. "Hey," I said, "do you see those boys in the red jerseys coming up the steps? Do you see number twenty-four? Say that to him!" Then I ran to my car as fast as I could.

Sure enough, as William walked up the steps with his team buddies—the presence of victory in their confident swaggers, lots of high fiving and smiling all around—the dad from the other team yelled over to my son, "Hey, number twenty-four!"

William and his buddies turned to see who had called out to the victorious one.

When the dad had the team's full attention, he pointed to William and yelled, "Be the sunshine!"

I laughed so hard I thought I would lose it. Even from my hiding place, I heard William yell above all the fun, "Mommm!"

Ever since those soccer games, the words "be the sunshine" has become the buzz phrase in our house. Those three words have come to mean so many different things. I kiss my kids and whisper to them on their way to school, "Go be the sunshine." The kids pop into my room while I pack for a trip and encourage me by saying, "Be the sunshine, Mom."

But most importantly and as a Christ follower, every day the phrase "be the sunshine" reminds me of my calling on this earth. Jesus spoke these words to you and to me, "Let your light shine before men" (Matthew 5:16 NASB). Then He said, "The righteous will shine like the sun in the kingdom of their Father" (Matthew 13:43).

He's talking about us. We are called to be the sunshine!

The LORD is God, and he has made his light shine on us.

PSALM 118:27

I Am Not the Light That Shines

The Christian does not think God will love us because we are good, but that God will make us good because He loves us. Just as the roof of a sunhouse does not attract the sun because it is bright, but becomes bright because the sun shines on it.

C.S. LEWIS

This morning I sit alone in my house. It's very quiet here except for an occasional barking dog and the gentle hum of the washing machine. As I linger for a few minutes to consider my own personal sunshine, I guess it's the quiet that begins to whisper the truth of who I am.

I am not so much actually. A simple woman. A pretty good wife. An imperfect mom with no idea what to make for dinner. Ordinary. Not so shiny on my own.

If I had gotten up this morning and tried to convince myself to be the sunshine, the truth is I would have pitiful little to offer this world. I am just a woman who follows Christ. Long ago I proved that I am not enough. I can't make my own light. I can't free myself from darkness. I need a Savior. Oh, my goodness, I need a Savior.

I am so grateful that the Bible is clear about where our light comes from. You don't have to be your own light, and neither do I. Look at how beautifully the Bible teaches us about the powerful light of God.

God is light.
The LORD is my light (Psalm 27:1).

Jesus, God's Son, is light.
I am the light of the world (John 8:12).

Followers of Jesus are given His light.
Whoever follows me will never walk in darkness,
but will have the light of life (John 8:12).

All we have to do is believe.
Believe in the light…so that you may become
children of light (John 12:36).

God fills our hearts with His light.
For God, who said, "Let light shine out of darkness,"
made his light shine in our hearts (2 Corinthians 4:6).

Jesus wants us to shine.
Let your light shine (Matthew 5:16).

We shine for God's glory.
That they may…glorify your Father
in heaven (Matthew 5:16).

When Jesus told His followers, "Let your light shine,"
He was talking about the light given to them when they
believe in Him as their Savior. No one has to go out
and find some light. Or pretend to be light. Or buy a
newfangled kind of light. Jesus was then—and still is—
the only light.

Jesus is saying to us today: I am the light, and when you
follow Me with your life, I'll put My light in your heart.
Let My light shine in all you do and every place you go.
I want this world to see My light through you. If you will
be the sunshine, My Father will be glorified.

*Come, house of Jacob, and let us walk
in the light of the LORD.*

ISAIAH 2:5 NASB

13

Learning
to Shine

When you speak of Heaven, let your face light up,
let it be irradiated with a heavenly gleam, let your eyes
shine with reflected glory. But when you speak of Hell—
well, then your ordinary face will do.

CHARLES H. SPURGEON

My daughter Taylor was about seventeen when we took a mother-daughter trip to New York. While there, the one thing my teenage girl really wanted was a big-city haircut. I had no idea where to go or who to call, so one afternoon I walked into a fancy looking hair salon near our hotel, asked if they could take a new client, and made an appointment for Taylor.

The next afternoon we made our way down to the salon. While Taylor got her hair cut, I waited in the lobby, but when I heard the stylist's blow-dryer, I wandered back to watch the final touches from a chair close to my daughter. From the time we entered the salon, every person had been gracious and kind to my baby girl.

While I sat there, an older man walked through the salon several times. He seemed important—a debonair gentleman if I had ever seen one. I later found out he had owned the salon for close to forty years.

"Is that your daughter?" he asked, motioning toward Taylor.

"Yes. We are taking a mother-daughter trip," I told him.

He kept looking at Taylor while he spoke to me. "She has a light around her," he said matter-of-factly.

"Excuse me?" I asked, not anticipating such a direct yet random observation.

"She has a light around her," he said matter-of-factly.

"She has a light around her. I see it each time I walk past her." Then he turned and looked at me. "Did you know she is covered in light?" he said as if he were telling me something I'd never heard.

I smiled and said, "I do know she is covered in light. There is light all around her. It comes from inside of her. We believe it's the light of Jesus Christ," It was my turn to stare at my baby girl who was just sitting there shining, completely oblivious to the conversation going on behind her.

The salon owner brushed aside my reference to Jesus and told me, "It's an aura. I rarely see someone with such a bright covering, but she has it."

I thanked him, agreed with his almost correct observation, and then silently prayed for him. *Oh, God, I pray this man heard me. The light he sees in my daughter is Your Son, Jesus. May he come to know the true source of light. It's You. Amen.*

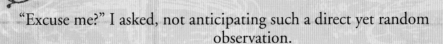

Though we left the salon with a New York hairdo, I also left with an ache in my heart. That sweet man, a complete stranger, was obviously crazy successful in business, incredibly insightful, spiritually searching, and yet so misguided. I have prayed for him many times in the years since we were there.

Here's the thing. I believe he did see a light around Taylor. For goodness sake, if you could meet her, you'd see it too. She is filled with the powerful indwelling of the Holy Spirit, and while she is just as big a sinner as her mama, she is completely in love with her Lord and Savior, Jesus Christ. Her very countenance is such a bright reflection of His presence in her soul. That girl shines!

But I don't think Taylor just woke up one day bright and shiny. I believe that she has learned how to shine. She longs to be a strong follower of Christ, and the pursuit of Him keeps turning up her light! It's called the journey of spiritual maturity.

In the book of 2 Corinthians, Paul explains what happens to followers of Christ like this: "But whenever anyone turns to the Lord, [darkness] is taken away" (3:16). "All of us, then, reflect the glory of the Lord with uncovered

We believe it's the light of Jesus Christ.

faces; and that same glory, coming from the Lord, who is the Spirit, transforms us into his likeness in an ever greater degree of glory" (3:18 GNT).

Maybe you can think of the light that comes from spiritual maturity this way. As we become mature followers of Christ (meaning we are learning to live and love as Jesus did), we are being transformed into the likeness of Christ (looking more and more like Him and less and less like the person we used to be). And as we are transformed, our very presence begins to reflect His light to this world with an ever increasing glory. (That means really shining!)

You and I are not manufacturers of light. We are only mirrors...

You and I are not manufacturers of light. We are only mirrors, little, tiny reflectors that send the light of Jesus out into darkness. Each one of us is learning what it really means to shine. Each light becomes ever brighter as we learn to love God more.

Are you growing in your knowledge of Jesus? Are you learning how to shine—which means acting like Jesus—wherever you've been assigned for this very day? Are you

- **quick to forgive,**
- **humble enough to serve in every kind of setting,**
- **generous in your giving,**
- **filled with compassion and action for the suffering,**
- **joyful in countenance,**
- **attentive and kind, and**
- **able to listen to the heavenly Father for guidance and wisdom?**

Are you learning to shine right where you are, no matter what circumstances come your way?

The LORD is my light and my salvation—
whom shall I fear?

PSALM 27:1

Hide It under a Bushel?

Some people are so much sunshine
to the square inch!

WALT WHITMAN

I've been humming an old camp song for days now. It goes something like this:

This little light of mine,
I'm gonna let it shine.
This little light of mine,
I'm gonna let it shine.
This little light of mine,
I'm gonna let it shine.
Let it shine,
Let it shine,
Let it shine.

Hide it under a bushel? No!
I'm gonna let it shine.
Hide it under a bushel? No!
I'm gonna let it shine.
Hide it under a bushel? No!
I'm gonna let it shine.
Let it shine,
Let it shine,
Let it shine.

The song actually comes from the very words of Jesus: "You are the light of the world. A city built on a hill cannot be hid. No one after lighting a lamp puts it under the bushel basket, but on the lampstand, and it gives light to all in the house. In the same way, let your light shine before others, so that they may see your good works and give glory to your Father in heaven (Matthew 5:14-16 NRSV).

When I hear people say, "My relationship with God is very private," I think to myself, *That may be true, but it appears to be so private that no one knows you are a follower of Jesus.* To hide your relationship with your Savior means that you are choosing to disobey His instructions. Jesus is very clear. We are supposed to shine!

He wants us to light up like a city on a hill.

His version of shining doesn't sound very private. He wants us to light up like a city on a hill, a city with a light so bright that people can see it from a long way off. He says we are supposed to be like a lamp that gives light to all in the house. The people we live with and encounter every single day are supposed to see the light of Christ in us.

I have a confession. Sometimes I hide the light Jesus gave me by crawling under a bushel and waiting for people to pass by. Other times I quietly hide my light beneath the basket until my situation requires less courage.

Almost every weekend I travel, and most of that travel is by airplane where I sit elbow to elbow with all kinds of people. I confess that for years I would do a million things while flying—read Christian books, look at newspapers, work on my computer, study from the Bible software on my iPad—but I would never pull out my thick, worn Bible and read it. No way would I plop that thing down on my knees, let the Bible ribbon fly, turn those pages I dearly love, and take God's Word fresh into my heart.

I honestly thought I was keeping the door open to have a conversation with my seatmates if I didn't read my Bible in front of them. Thinking that if they judged me before we ever spoke, I'd lose the opportunity to be the light. I finally came to realize most people don't want to talk anyway. My seatmates are rarely open to more than a polite hello. Several years ago Jesus told me to take my light out from underneath the bushel. Even if they don't talk to me, they will see it.

Sometimes people strike up a conversation with me when they see my Bible, and sometimes they fall instantly asleep. For me the point is obedience. Bushel baskets are not carry-on luggage. I am supposed to shine. And you are too.

Your word is a lamp for my feet,
a light for my path.
PSALM 119:105

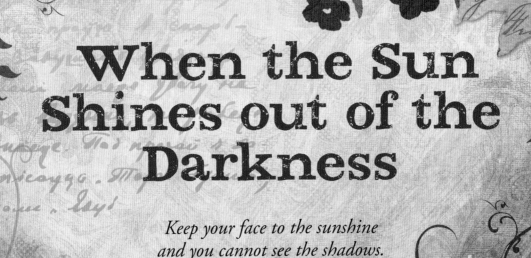

When the Sun Shines out of the Darkness

Keep your face to the sunshine
and you cannot see the shadows.

HELEN KELLER

I know a beautiful woman. She is both friend and inspiration. She has been living on this earth for thirty short years, and every single day of her thirty years, Mandy Young has been fighting to live.

I still remember the very first time I met Mandy. She was the blonde-headed, bright-eyed, effervescent woman coming down a hallway toward me, and it was her smile I saw first. She had the kind of smile that lit up the area. Then I noticed she was on crutches. Not so unusual. Eventually I realized this incredibly beautiful woman had only one leg. I wondered how a woman on crutches with only one leg could sparkle like that. Thankfully God introduced us, and I have come to understand how.

It turns out that having only one leg is the least of Mandy's struggles. Her journey so far has included more than a hundred hospitalizations, thousands of visits to many doctors, surgeries (including the one that took her hip and leg), and the nine times her family was told she would not live through the night. Her family and friends have cried more tears and prayed more prayers than anyone can imagine. And that sweet Mandy, she has endured every needle stick, each desperate prognosis, every bout of nausea and pain, and the endless poking, prodding, and pondering what to do next.

Mandy has been a research patient at the National Institutes of Health in Bethesda, Maryland for twenty-one years. After twenty years of studying her body, scientists decided that she is the only person in the world to have her specific genetic mutation, which produces a life filled with disease, illness, and infection. Can you even imagine?

But then you meet her, and nothing—I mean nothing—about the way she lives her life reveals even a hint of the darkness she has walked through. Mandy is a passionate follower of Jesus Christ. She is filled and bursting with the radiant light of His love for her.

Here's what Mandy says about her disease. "I know God gave me my disease for a reason; it's not for my purpose but for *His*. My life is not about me; unlike what my generation so wants us to believe, it's about *Him*! And knowing that *He* is in charge of my life, gives me hope for those things that seem so unclear, like my disease and living without answers for so many years."

Be joyful always.

1 Thessalonians 5:16 GNT

I tell you what, Mandy Young is in the sunshine business! She ought to give the rest of us shining lessons. I have never in my life encountered a light that shines from darkness so brightly.

I've realized that Mandy's taken God at His word. She trusts Him to keep His promises to her. She believes in His goodness. And she is determined to obediently follow His wisdom.

I struggled with a specific passage from Scripture for years. It's a little tiny verse that says this, "Be joyful always" (1 Thessalonians 5:16 GNT). It's God's word to us, but I've truly struggled with what sounds like a divine direct order. *Lord, are you sure? There is so much pain in this world. Darkness, suffering, loss, grief, sadness, disease, and genetic mutations.*

Are you sure that it's possible for a human being to really be joyful always?

Last summer I had the privilege of spending a few months tracing the word "joy" through the Bible. I researched and wrote and studied about joy for weeks on end. Finally I arrived at this very passage and this very strong command that surely wasn't meant to be taken so literally. Here is what I found out about, "Be joyful always."

In both the Hebrew and Greek languages, the word "joy" has two different meanings. The first meaning of joy is an emotion. We all understand that kind of joy. It's the sunny-day-everything's-going-my-way kind of joy. Easy-breezy joy. It's the emotion we feel when we're happy about something.

The second biblical meaning defines joy as something you choose to possess. It's a joy that is independent of your circumstances and your feelings. It has to do with a choice you make.

He told us to choose joy.

Do you want to guess which version of the word "joy" is found in the verse in 1 Thessalonians 5:16 in which we are instructed to "be joyful always"?

Yep. God did not stutter over these words. He did not ask us to feel mushy, cotton-candy like, and silly, giddy happy always. He told us to choose joy. It's a very grown-up, mature believer thing to do.

We might paraphrase this passage like this: No matter what is going on, no matter what you feel or don't feel, no matter if you understand or don't understand, choose to live and give and be filled with the joy of the Lord. Always. Every day. Every hour. Always.

I guess Mandy Young already knows all of that. Her beautiful life tells the world that she is walking through darkness on this earth, encountering setbacks and disappointments at every turn, but because she belongs to Jesus, she lets His love make her brave in the dark. She is choosing to be joyful always.

I think I'm going to make Mandy a T-shirt. The front will say, "You're looking at sunshine," and the back will read, "God is my light." I pray for that girl all the time, and after most of those prayers, I ask the Lord, *Teach me to shine like Mandy.*

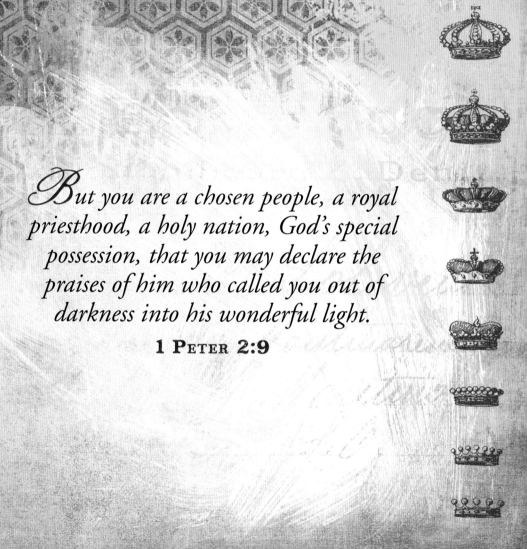

But you are a chosen people, a royal priesthood, a holy nation, God's special possession, that you may declare the praises of him who called you out of darkness into his wonderful light.

1 PETER 2:9

When the Darkness Doesn't Budge

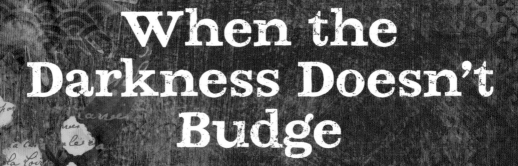

Let your light so shine before men, that others,
awed and charmed by the consistency of your
godly life, may come to enquire, and to say
you have been with Jesus.

WILLIAM MORLEY PUNSHON

Only God could do this.

About twenty minutes ago, my son Grayson came bursting through the backdoor after school. "Mom," he hollered to me.

"I'm in here, honey," I yelled back from my writing chair. "How was school?"

Around the corner he came, and with no earthly idea about what I'd been doing all day, he just said this to me—I am not kidding—"Mom, school was okay, but, Mom, you gotta know it is so hard to be the light at that school. I mean it. Every single day, I am completely surrounded by darkness. There is no way I will ever be enough light."

"Grayson, do you know what I've been sitting here doing?"

"No."

"I've been writing about our call to be God's light in the darkness."

"No way."

"Way."

Grayson went on to tell me that he's not personally discouraged about being just one of a few Jesus lights at his school. He's frustrated because no one seems to get it. The other students see his light. They respect his light. They have even given him two nicknames, "Jesus" and "Sunshine." (I told him I'd take either of those.) But Grayson doesn't see anything changing. He consistently shows up every day, bringing the light of Christ, but the darkness never seems to budge.

I hope that what I said to my son this afternoon will encourage you too. I told him something like this: "We are called to be obedient. We shine on assignment from God. Grayson, until graduation day you have been divinely assigned to that school, those teachers, and the thousands of students who go there. Your only responsibility is to reflect back to them what God has done for you. You do that with your voice, the words you choose, your work effort, your smile, your servant's heart, your compassion, and your grace. Baby, you just get yourself over there every morning and shine bright as the sun.

God has sent the Holy Spirit to take care of the change.

"God has sent the Holy Spirit to take care of the change. You are planting seeds in the hearts of young men and women. You are radically and gently speaking the truths of Scripture. You are boldly saying why you act the way you do and who the Lord of your life is. That is your assignment. The Holy Spirit will take care of the rest. You cannot hold the entire school in a holy headlock until they cry, 'Jesus!'

"You may never know how many people will one day remember your light or the name of Jesus and finally let the God of heaven set them free. But that's not your assignment. You're supposed to shine into their darkness. God loves them even more than you do, and He will keep coming with His radiant light for all who have eyes to see."

Maybe your assignment is a lot like Grayson's right now, surrounded by darkness with no change in sight. Can I give you some encouragement? God works in the unseen. Behind the scenes. Deep in the hidden places of the heart. If He has sent you and your light into darkness, then He is at work. Trust what you cannot see to the God who never misses a thing.

God is glorifying Himself. Let Him shine, baby. Let him shine.

Do everything without grumbling or arguing, so that you may become blameless and pure, "children of God without fault in a warped and crooked generation." Then you will shine among them like stars in the sky.

PHILIPPIANS 2:15

Delivering Sunshine

We are, by our very union with Christ, the light of the world.
As light, we are to shine in the world around us.
If you do not shine, you are not fulfilling your function;
worse than that, you are detracting.

C.R. WOOD

Books are my complete and total weakness. I often wander through airport bookstores between flights to make the rounds and see what's new. About a year ago, I found and purchased a book called *Delivering Happiness* in one of those bookstores. The truth is I only bought the book because of the title. That crazy powerful title made me walk all the way across the store, pick up the book, and thumb through the pages. I then put it down because I really didn't need another book. After I reached my gate, I turned right around and went all the way back to that store to buy the book. The title wouldn't leave me alone. Though the book was shelved among the zillions of business books, I had to know what kind of corporate ideology might be called "delivering happiness."

For at least six months, *Delivering Happiness* sat in my huge stack of books. I was content just to look over at the title every once in a while because it made me smile. I wasn't convinced that the business of Angela Thomas—which involved only part-time helpers and was quite possibly the tiniest business on the planet—qualified as business book material. Obviously the need to read such a book did not seem urgent.

One day I finally put that book in my travel bag and, over the next few days, read it cover to cover. Lickety-split. Underlined. Highlighted. Starred and circled. On every phone call home to my husband, I quoted the part I had just read. *Delivering Happiness* did something to me that weekend. As a person with a tiny business, I was incredibly inspired and motivated by the content. But even more powerfully, I felt deeply challenged about how I was living out my faith.

Delivering Happiness: A Path to Profits, Passion, and Purpose was written by Tony Hsieh, the CEO of Zappos.com, Inc. The book has become both a *New York Times* and *Wall Street Journal* bestseller. My only previous encounter with Zappos involved ordering a pair of shoes online for my son. The shoes didn't fit so I called to ask if I could return them. The nicest customer-service guy generously let me return the shoes, exchange them for another size, and then gave me free shipping for the whole deal. I remember being so impressed with him but assumed I had gotten lucky enough to talk to the one nice person who worked there. After reading the book, I now know that really great guy was only doing what he had been trained to do. He was delivering happiness.

Zappos operates the entire company and its culture based on the following core values:

1. Deliver **WOW** through service
2. Embrace and drive change
3. Create fun and a little weirdness
4. Be adventurous, creative and open-minded
5. Pursue growth and learning
6. Build open and honest relationships with communication
7. Build a positive team and family spirit

8. **Do more with less**
9. **Be passionate and determined**
10. **Be humble**

Here's what's interesting to me. In *Delivering Happiness*, Tony never makes any reference to faith, religion, or spirituality, which leaves the reader to assume faith has not been a guiding influence.

And yet the Zappos team landed squarely on many teachings of Scripture as they developed the core values of their company. Whether they know it or not, Scriptural values have built the foundation that makes their business successful. Augustine and Aquinas both taught, "All truth is God's truth," so that wherever you encounter truth, whether in science, business, or culture, you have encountered truth that belongs to God. Whatever is true in this world, points to God, and the source of that truth doesn't matter. Zappos claims to have discovered a path to profits, passion, and purpose, when in fact they have discovered many ancient and true teachings from the Bible.

Here's where I am deeply challenged. As followers of Jesus Christ, we have the corner on these principles. We have a heavenly Father who loves us. We have the Holy Spirit to guide us. We have forgiveness of our sins. Eternal security. The hope of heaven. The light of Christ. Joy everlasting. We, the followers of Christ, ought to be delivering joy to this world. Delivering passion. Delivering sunshine. As a matter of fact, we ought to out-deliver times eternity!

I'm thrilled for the Zappos people. I hope I get to meet Tony one day and share a cup of coffee and an exciting conversation, but his book did not compel me to become a Zappos groupie. This book made me lean into God and thank Him for the beautiful truth He has already given to us in the Bible. Everything we build on *His* truth is for *His* glory, and what is done for *His* glory will shine!

God's truth has the power to change this world if we build our lives on it...

Delivering Happiness did inspire me to turn up my shine, because I really want this world to know who Jesus is. Happiness is fleeting, and the profits will fade. Our purpose is greater. We have the privilege of delivering God's everlasting joy to a world that desperately needs it. Go figure. I never expected so many spiritual lessons from a secular business book.

God's truth has the power to change this world if we will build our lives on it and fill our hearts with it. Stand on the hill where you have been called. And let His truth shine.

For you were once darkness,
but now you are light in the Lord.
Live as children of light.

EPHESIANS 5:8

Our Mission

Light gives of itself freely, filling all available space. It does not seek anything in return; it asks not whether you are friend or foe. It gives of itself and is not thereby diminished.

MICHAEL STRASSFELD

Before the coming of Jesus, there was a man named John the Baptist. His mission on earth was to point to Jesus. "There was a man sent from God whose name was John. He came as a witness to testify concerning that light, so that through him all might believe. He himself was not the light; he came only as a witness to the light. The true light that gives light to everyone was coming into the world" (John 1:6-9).

John the Baptist was sent by God to be a witness to the light of Jesus. He never performed a miracle. He did not write a book in the Bible. His sole mission was to be a witness to the light.

His sole mission was to be a witness to the light.

I believe that is exactly your mission and mine. John the Baptist was a voice in the desert that caused people to think about Jesus. He was only one voice. One simple man with a very simple life. He was not the light, but he knew the light. And he told everyone he met about the coming light of Jesus. I don't get the impression that John the Baptist was afraid to be the only light in the darkness he encountered. Even alone, his security came from the truth he proclaimed.

Our mission is to use every resource entrusted to us to point to Jesus, to reflect His light, to point to His light, and to shine full of His light. "Then the righteous will shine like the sun in the kingdom of their Father" (Matthew 13:43).

Our mission is to use every resource entrusted to us to point to Jesus, to reflect His light, to point to His light, and to shine full of His light.

Righteousness and justice are the foundation of your throne; love and faithfulness go before you. Blessed are those who have learned to acclaim you, who walk in the light of your presence, Lord.

PSALM 89:14-15

May I Introduce You?

Dare to reach out your hand into the darkness,
to pull another hand into the light.

NORMAN B. RICE

Before we turn the last pages of this book, I have to tell you the most important thing. It is impossible to be the sunshine until you have invited Jesus to remove your darkness and fill your life with His light.

Who is Jesus? Who is the Son of God? Though we all walk in darkness, our souls long for the light. Though we long to be filled, nothing in this world delivers an everlasting light or gives an everlasting peace apart from the presence of Jesus. If you've already searched for light in a million other places, you know what I'm telling you is true.

It's my honor to introduce you to the glorious light of Jesus Christ. You see, God created you for His love. He desires a loving relationship with you. But God is holy, and we are not. The Bible says that God's holiness cannot have a relationship where there is sin. We all have sin.

So God, from the depths of His great love, sent His Son, Jesus, to pay for our sin. When Christ died on the cross, God said the punishment we deserved had been paid in full. Jesus' death saves us from the penalty of our sin. All our sin. Forever.

A prison guard who is mentioned in the Bible asked this question to Paul and Silas, "Sirs, what must I do to be saved?"

God created you for His love.

They replied, "Believe in the Lord Jesus, and you will be saved" (Acts 16:30-31).

The same is true for us. When we believe in Jesus, our sins are forgiven, and we are saved from the punishment we deserve.

To believe is to become a follower of Christ and a member of the family of God. For all who follow Him, God sends the light of the Holy Spirit. Darkness is removed. Sin is forgiven. Eternal life is assured.

Darkness is removed. Sin is forgiven. Eternal life is assured.

If today you decide to follow Jesus Christ, then today is the day of your salvation. To begin to follow Jesus, pray to Him. You can pray with your own words. However you talk to Him is wonderful and completely sufficient because He is the one who understands your heart.

I also want you to know that Jesus is not like us. He is not wishy-washy with His love. He does not play games with your heart. He does not move the target that you aim for. When you believe, you belong to Him. And your new life begins—in the light. "I have come into the world as a light, so that no one who believes in me should stay in darkness" (John 12:46).

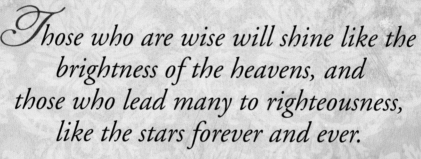

Those who are wise will shine like the brightness of the heavens, and those who lead many to righteousness, like the stars forever and ever.

DANIEL 12:3

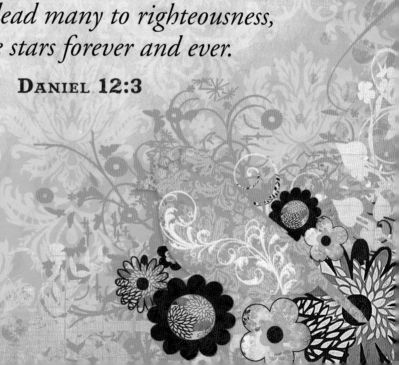

The Cave and the Sun

Once upon a time a cave lived under the ground, as caves have the habit of doing. It had spent its lifetime in darkness. It heard a voice calling to it: "Come up into the light, come and see the sunshine."

The cave retorted: "I don't know what you mean; there isn't anything but darkness."

Finally the cave ventured forth and was surprised to see light everywhere.

Looking up to the sun the cave said: "Come with me and see the darkness."

The sun asked: "What is the darkness?"

The cave replied: "Come and see."

One day the sun accepted the invitation. As it entered the cave it said, "Now show me your darkness!"

But there was no darkness.

AUTHOR UNKNOWN

And the moral of this little story is this:
**Where there is light, there can be no darkness.
Live in the light given to you by the Son of God.
The darkness hides when you shine.**